SELECTED POETRY BOOK VIII

NEUTRINO CANZONIERI EPIGRAMME INVESTIGATION 21ST CENTURY POETRY

PAUL SHAPSHAK, PHD

authorHOUSE

AuthorHouse™
1663 Liberty Drive
Bloomington, IN 47403
www.authorhouse.com
Phone: 833-262-8899

Published by AuthorHouse 05/08/2023

ISBN: 979-8-8230-0793-1 (sc)
ISBN: 979-8-8230-0792-4 (e)

Library of Congress Control Number: 2023908880

Print information available on the last page.

For my wife, Solveig

Anonymous aphorisms

Dyson, Kardashev, Sagan, Drake, Gold, and then...

Heedless amidst neutrinos

Neutrino catcher, oscillation, the long-look pitched, from goneby days.

Space-time traveler, beware syntax, context, idiom.

Contents

List of Illustrations

Book cover Art and Art photograph numbers 1-6, 8-12,
and 21-25 by Sir Rene Shapshak.

PART I

PASTORAL

Canzone 303

Pastoral Pacere

Thought consecrate disposition
Quell quote quorum
Align Elgin bolster
Placid temperate media
Transform
Consideration
Devote temper
Outlook
Allay
Appropriation
Estimate
Arrogation

Epigramme 311

Everyday

Willful zoned
Yore chactid wild fate
Whither wrought
Whisper wrought
Whilst wrong
Folly wrought
Whereof haughty
Fennel bergamot chicory
Wherefrom

Epigramme 315

Lintels

Threads hall
Truant Pandora
Threefold trophy
Apples golden

Epigramme 321

Unforeseen Groves

Pergolas
Distant greens bowers
Stress stroll sleep sloth
Panther aside
Tiger abounding unexpected
Assessment combination
Bowers

Canzone 311

Bergamot

Quiet things
Dispositions placid
Promoted rancor
Décor
Chicory basis decorous
Endorsed decorum
Confluence effects
Demuredness
Didactic erudition persuaded
Inobtrusive equable serene
Abstruse imperturbability
Upheld equable

Epigramme 320

Selected

Vex'd vest'd dross
Trifl'd circumscribed tried
Tread trelice treat
Stride treasure
Vexed violet villa
Vest vassal perplexed

- Paul Shapshak, PhD -

Epigramme 312

Shropshire

Field strew folk flowers
Golden sunsets stark sunrises
Have a nice day
Door open door shut
Translation language
Smoke steam dark dank narrows
Blended airs here there
Shored banks
Severn swift skylark
Saw-wing martin abrupt
Flight upward dream bound

Canzone 305

Guileless Obscurities

Pencill'd robotics
Top bottom
Charm strange
Up most down
Amethysts cavern
Splendid wheat fields daily
Sleuths crystal sculptured
Hadron trackers mythological wall
Receipts regards
Barley rye cantaloupe
In time now tomorrow
Next recolte deceits
Recalled recalled
Retrospect regardless
Irk beneath hard nine
May beckons sumer in
Swallows wrens
Eaves cheep
Sunder'd lightning clouds thunder'd
Rendered timely fostering care
Out lagoon depths
Remarked passing room to room
Among chambers stood ages
Year leaving last
Migratory unincidentals

Epigramme 317

Jonquil

Well by Idrunn
Ibises quench far
Flung flights ornamental
Storks seasons
Octaves fifths
Extravagant
Fourths augmented
Forth first and firm by Severn

Epigramme 313

Peal

Heightened lark
Swallow swoop
Day dividend
Rising attend
Dusk at end
Repetitive
Stay

Canzone 307

Deliberations

Elliot	Pound
Behan	Baez
Ben Canaan	Abelard
Chatterton	Pushkin
Lermontov	Joyce
Blake	Donne
Brecht	Schiller
Brontës	Dickens
Browning	Barrett-Browning
Burns	Milton
Byron	Wordsworth
Christina Rossetti	Dante Rossetti
Dante	Edda
Khayyam	Sappho
Dickinson	Weavers
Ekelof	Froding
Empedocles	Villon
Esenin	Ukrainskaya
Ferlinghetti	Chaucer
Goethe	Fitzgerald
Graves	Virgil
Grimm	Froding
Heine	Petrarca
Housman	Tennyson
Immanuel the Roman	Ibsen
King James	Li Po
Kazantzakis	Jong

Ferlinghetti	King Richard I
Keats	Shelley
Li Bo	Halevi
King David	King Solomon
Lady Murasaki	Basho
Longfellow	Kipling
Lorca	Neruda
Millay	Zarathustra
Ovid	Frost
Poe	Thomas
Pushkin	Lermontov
Rimbaud	Nemerov
Scott	Widsith
Shakespeare	Marlowe
Spenser	Sidney

Canzone 309

Measured

Strindberg	de France
Sturlison	Langland
Undset	Millay
Vedas	Southy
Wilmot	Vyasa
Yeats	Tagore
Cherrelles	Supremes
Fats Domino	Housman
M'nM	Snoopdog
Lewis	Notorious B.I.G.
Gould	Menuhin
Heifetz	Einstein
Scarlatti	Bach
Buxtehude	Palestrina
Zuckerman	Des Pres
Barenboim	Handel
Haydn	Schweitzer
Hilbert	Tupac
LLCoolJ	Blondie
Perlman	Hahn
Michelangeli	Milstein
Bell	Elman
Ricci	Oistrakh
Paganini	Francescatti
Haendel	Kogan
Milstein	Fischer

Canzone 304

Guardian

Carnelian amethyst
Ruby diamond topaz
Sapphire cerulean
Aquamarine emerald
Not nefandous frore
Beneath cobalt skies
Nimble azure
Indigo ill absent
Unaccompanied
Not abandoned
Adze chisel block
Additional aera

Epigramme 319

Brookland

Poplars cedars yews
Ash winds windows chime
Clocked elsewhere light
Arrow heightened dissociated
Inscribed scope far distant
Domains allocated

Epigramme 318

Time's Parsimony

Unlearned time stretched
Time's unlettered disbursement
Improvident time-spread
Time's game spent bundled
Time's thrift fringe
Spared-time far-flung

- Paul Shapshak, PhD -

Epigramme 314

None Today

Markings
Again
Away

PART II

MYTHOLOGY

René Shapshak

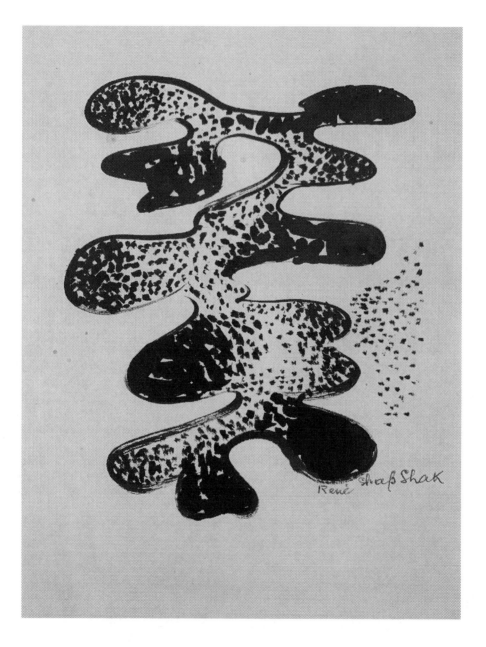

René ShapShak

3½ Inches

Epigramme 322

Mythos

Scriabin Mozart
Rimsky-Korsakoff
Haydn Bach
Buxtehude breath
Poplar magnolia elm
Myrtle Freud
Jung Glinka
Philosophe
Mirth breadth
Zelda sephirah
Zephyr

Epigramme 316

Well

Then Mimir
Atte
Shade Yggdrasil
Nine worlds
Nine roads
Nine gates
Nine steps
From Heimdall
Imparted

Canzone 308

Draupnir

Shade
Yggdrasil
Daina Dvalin
Duneyr Durathor
Worlds eaves
Bridge-roads
Self-contained consists
Nine-fold ways means
Gadfly Mjolnir handles
Light-thought Eastre
Gaard enthrall roundabout
Providence
Loki

Canzone 306

Syzygy

Sylvan dreams
Forest shadow
Meadow larks
Bulls bellow
Mountain crags
Dales swallow
Abyss acknowledgements
Searches thorough brow
Fulminant acquisition
Consequently concluded escarpment

- Paul Shapshak, PhD -

Canzone 305

Tangent

Shrouded mystery
Understood toward escarpments
Indemonstrable
Zoroastrian proclamation
Rolling cylinder
Day portended
Remain scripts

Epigramme 341

Thrall

Surfeit vicissitudes
Tine studies threads
Things syzygies
Thralls halls
Thorn configurations
Thoughts
Naught

Epigramme 340

Ardent

Imprint
Lest
Keen
Create circle
Spiral glide
Glimmer glim
Inscribe
List
Case
Provoked calm
Disquieted parallax
Contravariant
Contravene
Impose
Dressed

Canzone 321

Muse

Lieless mountain-tops
Limit mountainous
Ninefold oblation loss obdurate
Muse life-line

- Paul Shapshak, PhD -

Epigramme 323

Rg Vista View

Proviso
Prompt plench
Pass collaged
Patchwork rig
Palencq locks
Finch work

Epigramme 315

Altruist

Hummingbird sparrow finch robin
Blue squirrel chipmunk homeland
Insisted equitable equity
Inevitable inviolacy

- Paul Shapshak, PhD -

Epigramme 328

Loki's View

Norm gauntlet
Mjolnir
Truth pounder
Severe avenger
Asunder

Canzone 313

September

September's migrant reamer's
Post-haste recoltes
Portcullises embroiled schemes
Dual shrouds pondering
Schooling absent pitiless
Clouds renowned
Remarked again
Stand stand respite
Time ago bended
Steel'd stealth
Another aera soliloquy
Gone by another time

- Paul Shapshak, PhD -

PART III

COSMOLOGY

Canzone 317

Imitation Brands

Cataracts conversant terminal moraines
Loomed hover pretense
Charades hurtled
Thunders lighting motion sound
Actions added day another realm
Most extra time
Minkowskian laguerrian polynomial
Lorentz bees staggered dance
Space-time immemorial
Polysyllabic algebras startled
Mirror Noether symmetries
Frank fraught foster inwalled mirror
Foes eloquence elated ersatz
Blooms blossoming among starlings
Thinking swift swallows
Star gazing larks

Canzone 319

Counter Caged Hypothetic

Barisani von Ployer
Count Thun Stadler Salieri
Da Ponte von Weber Leutgeb
Gottfried van Swieten
Hambacher Domenica
Hummel Haydn
Mesmer von Walsegg
Natschibintschibi
Ramm von Puchberg
Schack von Jacqin
Whom else

Canzone 318

Mirabilis Elements

Anno mirabilis
Photons atoms
Special relativity
Questions questions questions
Citizens atoms psych
Placed here there
Constitutional
Culprit time
Cupid's arrows
Sync forward
Hard core humanist
200,000 years traversed
Light speed

Epigramme 314

Light Speed

Slowed halted demeaned
Destiny 200,000 years
Continuum hypothesized
Discrete
Dared
Darned

Epigramme 339

Circumstance

Placed stature
Instance conscribed
Yesterday ornamentally
Yesteryear climatic
Apples cranberries
Fallen netted trucked
Traversed continents
Diverged content averr'd

Entanglements

At distance
Detach, remote, vast
Altitude
Elevation lofty highness
Replete respect repositioned
Spatial sub-space
Extra-dimension isospin
Portcullis lintel
Hedged hedgerows
Recumbence recombinant
Restitutive result
Desultory distractions
Manifest manifolds
Marvelous minuets pirouettes
Presages presentations
Ocular blended
Entanglements
EPR smiles laser lights
The bells bone-by
Aftermath Methuselah mighty hunter
Lamech, Jared, Enoch
More than a day
Journey beyond reaches
Scope unfathomed
Crested views hidden
In plain sightings

- Paul Shapshak, PhD -

Epigramme 343

Bell Shells

Alejandro Scarlatti
Resonances clatter
Gravitational reverberations
Echo aftershocks
Circadian pulses
Palpitations
Rhythms
Unwielded stayed entered
At door at edge at embraided
Embroided warp
Woof dichotomy syzygy
Consequently connective
Consecutive

Canzone 316

Pall Mall

Confluencing
Resounds Montezuma's palace Micchu Picchu
Differing differentiate planets tide five rivers Kush
Propounds Mohenjodaro Harappa Lothal Kalibangan
Dholavira Rakhargari
Birds land midst
Linden elms oaks yews magnolias
Cyrus cylinder
Scripts iconographies
Indus
Indus Ganges
Gangetic plain
Forty days nights

Canzone 315

Getting There

Gauss
Electric field
Magnetic field
Integral
Surface
Volume element
Faraday
Ohm
Oersted
Lentz
Maxwell
D'Alembertian
Laplace
Double gradient
Curvature
Benjamin Franklin EM
Storm investigations
Fields

Canzone 330

Star Gaze

Forge barn field
Tractor tractate
Croupier loom
High above
Crowds mad irate
Far meadow
Scale set balance
Book star weights

Epigramme 331

Knots Gauges

Field circulate
Cosh sine laws
Distribute
Flux alteration
Ampere Maxwell Faraday Ohm
Permeability transformation
Permittivity alteration
Boundaries potential
Reiteration nevertheless
Density waves
Recurrence
Current Laplacian
Reappearance
Divergent spaces
Gradient matters
Curled metric
Guardian

Epigramme 333

Starlight

Near measures
Constants
Star efforts fear
Perished thoughts
Evanescently quiet
Traversed surprised
Transparency jonquil
Bliss daylight tranquil
Steps

- Paul Shapshak, PhD -

Canzone 331

Virtue

Prior
Couched lotus
Stork crane
Leaf turnover
Advantage
Release rest
Hedge reserves
Means windbrake
Stellar configurational
Field superposition
Ginungagap
Changeling
Galactic cluster

Canzone 335

Gauge

Field equations action
Invariant transform added
Quantum mechanics partition
Obstruct hurdle
Barricade Lorenz dimension latitude
Electrodynamics measure
Yang Mills factor
Isotopic spin isospinor
Transitory transition
Momentless momenta
Blockade Boson

Epigramme 324

Migratory Bosons

Explanatory paths
Evanescent connections
Expository orations
Prime curvature manifolds
Veiled trek
Conformal mapping
Jest beneath pall
Cloaked forces between
Cryptic existent actuality

Epigramme 334

Neutrino Electromagnetics

Neutrino enigma
Vertex current
Gauge Lorentz
Four form factor
Current matrix
Dirac vanished dipole
Majorana magnetic
Electric form evaporate
Banished CP reels
Pulled charged
Nonstandard evanescent
Charged radius finite
Existence
Resonant spin-flavor
Exceeds altogether

- Paul Shapshak, PhD -

Epigramme 335

Gauge

Transubstantiated
Coordinate independent
Self-govern
Untouched motion
Besides seeing
Unseen unbeknownst
By point invariant
Points potential
Vector messenger
Allow symmetry
Spin isospin
Invariant some days

Epigrammaton 336

Cryptic

Boson
Matter darkened
Veiled reality
1935

PART IV

THEOLOGY

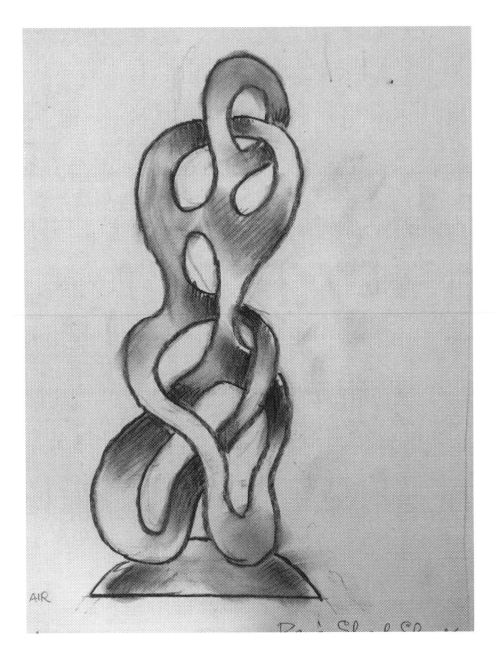

AIR

Epigramme 411

Lest Coast

Stones glow glowering
Stave staff staffing
Mown grass mowing
Cleft deftly clarting
Clot deft daubing
Sheep by moonlight
Tread trample treading
Dearth hedgerows draft
Draft hedging breadth

Canzone 449

Ersatz Chronicle

Flowing quoth
False being tide
Drift fallow
Incorrect Fair-floss
Fall flourish
Fair fallow
Eyes wraiths
Flimsy assembled
Wending wrecked
Wend wreaths clustered
Well-contented wrang
Weep wroth
Desist discontinuity

- Paul Shapshak, PhD -

Epigramme 457

Plough

Sumer arrive concierge
Patina consequent mode
Verité isolations quotients
Capacious plant corridors
Shore river sea ocean uproar
On waters calm day
Dusk
Beneath sensor
Pastures paddocks
Hommocks denes dells
Opaque fields

Canzone 413

Spring

Forgotten hills
Far-off calls refrains
Engulfed rain
Drained marsh
Betwixt bewildered
Unceased parsed
Far away sight
Seen grange harvest
Halsted Wentlock stead
Algebra Lie Ricci Tensor
Sheaths sheaves shelters
Archer

Canzone 403

Indolence

Fruit bearer integrity virtue valor
Integral labor service amenity facility intensified
Dressed trees bear merit encouraged
Goodness land sea ocean vista
Winters' fires leap cosmic brinies
Doubt distended complacent village spam
Kalidasa mile
Dared delibly indolent lions
Deliberate lionesses aggregate congressed

Epigramme 479

Villon

Song lay
Slow even
Smote sounds
Sonorous sorts
Speechless spent
Our hours ours'
Matins
Unspent spirited
Spread
Spur poised
State star
Untarnished bloom
Unblemished color
Reasoned unreasoning
Respites unrested calms
Steeped stepped flying
Stabled stall spirited
Apparated sanctioned
Inviolabilities
Inviolables
Infringeabilities
Concluded
Books of hour

- Paul Shapshak, PhD -

Epigramme 481

Neutrino

Forlorn nothing
All Majorana
Seized double beta
New-found luster lofty
Obfuscated oblivia
Sea keel Pompei

Epigramme 415

Veneer-Shine

Vassalage trelice
Treat veneer
Treasure dispatch
Vassal tread
Veneer-glow

- Paul Shapshak, PhD -

Epigramme 407

Sometime

Erstwhile desiderata
Drafted dim vocal
Iterable intrinsic formed
Summer drafts
Drawn scapes scattered
Wheat chaff stalks
Golden downdraughts
Discerned

Canzone 451

Majorana

Pencil-praise help ingratiate
Pressed preservedly
Majorana presag'd
Dual symmetric neutrinos
Tied untied cycled
Fields found folks between
Fells vales paired
Misty dales hills pared
Patience dells press'd
Preposterous travels denes
Travails marvell'd
Makeless pearls press'd
Unmatched markers
Paradise parading pursuants
Domains dual

- Paul Shapshak, PhD -

PART V

HISTORY

Epigramme 483

Rescind

Upon recall windy day
Serviced retract time goneby
Consequent repeal attendences
Reserved reeves revoke

Canzone 487

Palette

Symmetry parallels
Circuitous calculus
Calcitonin epochs
Soft shells
Shells halves
Sealooks seares
Darnels hidden by
Clays by days dispositions by nights
Next day new

Epigramme 487

Providence

Folly's retribution
Firstly choate folly
Clouded cloistered
Cordon ed barricade
Obstructed obstacle
Farrow grange folded
Falter farm foist
Falsest foiled
Falsely foil

Epigramme 493

Enlightenment

Categorically
Ten
Many more
Mountains
Pericles Athens
Gaius Julius Caesar Rome
Hastings entangled
Magna Carta
Enlighten'd
Rights Spirit Law
Runnymede

Canzone 479

Forthright

Shrewsbury island streams
Dialectics far gone bridges
From distant tramples sharp gleams
Morning flares
Waving gone bys
Hills sheltering marshes
Silence provoked not at all

Epigramme 491

Grammar

Lilly rose field
Laurel trance
Joist pendulum
Plumb level
Aligned night
Barrel coop stable
Daybreak afternoon tea
Dawn reaper gathering
Harvest assembly
Not inaudible

- Paul Shapshak, PhD -

Epigramme 401

Cressy

Sky longbow
Rain gazed azured tint
Crecy day collapsed
Cressid steeped tent
Epaulettes characteristic
Greaves gauntlets seared
Kaleidoscope mottled tone
Greys greens orange grove
Arc-en-Ciel day preponderant
Rebuke
Restore
Resolve
Ivy walls straddling century
Goneby
Foregone

Epigramme 413

Dispositions

House climate   domestic atmosphere
Falls river chasms   tides vanished
Lords ladies   zoomed
Jezebel   assemblages
Enthralled throngs   neighbors
Collectors   iniquitous
Coveted   ambiguities
Tattered   volitions
Daylights   restored
Depositions   preferences
     Conflagrations
       Confabulations
         Relegated
           Regulated
Appended

- Paul Shapshak, PhD -

Canzone 497

Cast

Lilly daffodil primrose
Durst thieving magpie
Upon heath
Lava molten shift among rocks
Live molted snake
Beknownst cask echo

Canzone 499

Stedfast

Endure sullen diversion
Sultry set contentment
Dust situated counter
Home hence hindrance
Tasked unbeknownst
Gifted worthies
Canonical camelia
Cypress myrtle
Yew boxwood vinca majore
Poplar pine fir marginal
Marigolds rosemarys
Morning glories opening day
Night blushes ere dawn
Majorana journey
Patronage

- Paul Shapshak, PhD -

Canzone 339

Heine

Loreley
Mnemosyne Apollinaire
Breathe sway fortune providential
Nearby interweaved destiny amalgamated
Fell uttermost conference
Compassionateness gravity
Abandoned descant harmony
Sirin beatitude
Bold music lyred prohibitive
Frequencies perseverant trances
Encoded tolled incidences
Tension tress freefallen befell

Dreamt unfaded balsam
Clime folk-tales resorgimento
Rising tides practiced wade lochs
Betides cypress poplar thyme tarn

Aforementioned prior portended
Rien reins snow mist enclosed

Epigramme 321

Where

Galleries years
Poplars beckoning
Bolder day gleam
Belonging mindful
Besieged Innisfree
Awakened past
Infractions multiplied
Divided reciprocal
Reciprocity

Canzone 457

Marble

Pursuant preambles
Au courage au courage
Incourteous credibilities
Agate granite
Graffiti notwithstand
March's pressures
Marbled feats
Before July's persuance

PART VI

SOCIAL

Epigramme 406

Wrinkled Wherefore

Where-through fold
West-gate quietitudinously
Forthright kindlinesses
From gone-by
Frolik golden-stance
Friend lowered
Agglomeratedly fresh

Epigramme 414

Desk

Shires
Queen saved
Stand by
Loquaciously bright
Teeming fellows
By river
Dale
Hill and meadow
Seven and nine
Linden breezes
Miles seen

Canzone 466

Wend

Laurels wrecks

Wrackful weep

Wraiths Wax

Waters worthy

Juncture concatenations

Worth wastes

Violet vocabularies

Indigo lilac

Chrysanthemums

Morning glories

For it

Lances

Debates

Well-contented wrang

Weary labyrinth

Wrack wax worthy

Waterfall catacomb

Stage link short

Worthier trophies

Wilt votary wind

Mauve lavender

Nasturtiums

Flowering tillandias

Reasons

Spoken

Rendered

Canzone 473

Land

Country lakesides
Planetary cadets
Reveille awakened
Towering across
Planetary nebulae
Clay sand loam
Still earth
Quietitudes afternoons reveries
Pastures fenced stay sty-marked

Canzone 432

Hills

Idyllic meadows
Larks swoop
Surf meadow
Sunrise cast Vestavia hills
Mountain forest
Oak maple
Height

Epigramme 411

Shire

Yeoman shod
Corridor aslant
Twixt AngloSaxon learning
Norman obscurity
Avid blitzkrieg
Danelaw paid stand-offs
Mesmerized eschewn
Jungian sub-consciousness
Ingenuous unknown
Eluding contravention
Litigious escarpments
Estuaries estimates
Evidentiary excesses
Relegated cowpen
Pigsty stable-gate
Widsith to Langland
Yellow daffodil purple crocus
Bluebell iris
Orchards apple
Remembrances severe
Time unsevered
Earthen restrained
Landscapes

Epigramme 420

Asides

Sticky wicket
Curve ball
Spin aerodynamic
Interleaved unleavened
Sojourn's summer
Twilight's dusk
Bolt Apache bow
Digressions alive
State's ward
Intrusions dark
Dank spirits
Apprenticed brow
Opal day
Relics

Epigramme 477

Lie

Willing glad
Sobriety distraught
From Clununford shredded
Clun epiphenomena
Thames impossible shadows
Colors hewn marble granite stark
Raven nest kindred dread subtle
Creak through garden glad
Garrulous hapries
London ash provoke
Onyx yews press
Time poplars

Epigramme 470

Winds Change

Depth deflection
Counting chasms
Deep oceans
Cranes ibises egrets swans
Ducks towering storks
Perception tick birds
Condescension
Revise reedited
Reformulated
Resuscitated
Restoration remodeled
Regardless refinement

Canzone 430

Mill On The Severn

Exhortation star scholarship
Stare inquisitively
Stark fires via study step
Through prosaicism instantly
Jung mental metal myth
Instinctive restraint
Long-term memory
Sheared fleece
Snared psychology
Majorana moments binary
Key standard models oscillatory
On beams scathing
Glissando de capo
Skates confounded
Dismay baring counseling
Bearings misperceivedly
Bands merry forests well-trod
Dusk dawn work prevailed
Veiled work shire fonts hilly
At castle gates moot moats

- Paul Shapshak, PhD -

Canzone 501

Imputed Accreditations

Convey precipitous
Divisions bear
Whisper branch
Door by door
By branch fir cedar
Snow tranquil
Proximate dawn
Quiet today not
Yesterday tomorrow

Canzone 312

Credits

Heuristic seal
Scone stone
Blythe scope

Scorn
Seabound
Scythe

Blunt tiring pacific vista
Separate hammered
Seep semblance
Sessions by day
Dusk slumber
Mechanism night regain

Epigramme 511

Concerning

Vicissitude ensued
Compromise
Thread traced
Between Traced
Undivided
Concede concert

Epigramme 311

Veneer Disparity

Veneer-shine vex
Veneer-glow beam
Veneer vassalage
Vassal discrepancy
Incongruity ingenou
Soothed vantage
Shields incentives

- Paul Shapshak, PhD -

Canzone 511

Tract

Willfully zoned   Yore willful
Wild yore mazes   Whither wrought
Whisper wronged   Whilst wrought
Wrongs whereofs   Wherefrom wrinkle
Off mediated   Meditations quieten'd
Wherefores wrinkle   Vassal travesty
Variationed travail   Trail vantage
Rights straight'n'd   Aways deepen
Vantaged tractates   Vanquish'd quiet'd

Epigramme 310

Festive

Set pearls marigolds
Diamonds sapphires
Glass crystal
Chrysanthemums
Rubies amethysts
Pencill'd-in pen-ink
Marvel pressed
Masked Vestal
Invisible threads
Clotho Lachesis Atropos
No thread before it's time
No fire before
Gathering tent
Clouds mists fogs
Of place struck learned
Industrious unearthed
Office mayst
Conflagration radiated
Conflagrated firestorm
Burnt memento memes
Monoclasticism monotone
Polyphone resolved
Designed harmony
Tierce de Picardie
Embellished druthers
Thrice twice stepped
Storms mists
Rather relatively

PART VII

ECONOMICS

Canzone 302

Dynamics

Stanch holder portion
Conscripted consequence scupper
Shropshire Empire empirical impervious
Blockade brocade ambuscade
Repository fount excavate
Elgin Byron Blake
Rossettis Barrett Browning
Perused read
Menuhin Einstein Block
Scanned land browsed
Voyaged voiced voyeur over
Repossessed
Returned
Recalled
Educed recollected
Adduced randomly
Attained managed
Fortunato obligato

Epigramme 537

Thrived

Unbred stops
Tillage cordials
Time timorous
Uneared dues
Time thrift
Garnished slips
Unerred disunengauged
Time adrift
Ceilings haphazard

- Paul Shapshak, PhD -

Canzone 507

Hedgerow Walls

Beccons beacons bon
Beacons primed hedged
Bits pieced left-overs
Capital lost housemice
Dawn less dusky eventides
Else elsewhere become
Evade first light
Excess effort
Excess time
Field left-overs
Clave unto
Forsake warpen warden
Additions day night incipient
Expectation working
Time space bits
Labor vanity battling
Primed hedges endured upended
Savonarola charms eventide
Speaks charm conveyor belts
Taxes beatific tapped
Wane want winter-freeze
Want waste worth
Wardrobe Vesta virtue
Warrant whither whether vistas
Warranties with primes
Warrantless wonder
Habitat worn veneration
The law heretofore command
Interdiction

Epigramme 309

Today Directly

By the by
Serene Shropshire
Cherrelles bourgeon
Empires tennis
Winch weary
New day new dream
Bourgeois racquet
Abundance occasioned
Told folks afield
Oligarque barques
Stellar shadows'
Simple paths dendritic
Connections constancy
Cuminum cyminum cinnamon
Volition CP violation voluntary
Valor anti-particles anti-worlds
Magnetic fields tied tight binded
Sheaves' field dance linear

- Paul Shapshak, PhD -

Canzone 437

Exposé Chaotique

Frenzied glee
Flora gloat frantic
Glistened smirk
Frailty frank shimmer
Gilded fragility
Frailly imperfection
Frail gleam
Fractious glazed
Glower fox-smile veneer
Iridescent coat
Many invisibilities
Rocks ladders memories
Preternatured wings spheres disks
Found glass-marble
Forward-stride afforded glass
Forward afford
Fortune affordingly
Gild glass fortune
Fortune gilded-affirmingly
Fortune gilded-hope
Gilding fortune heralded
Crystalline transparencies

Epigramme 308

Antique Providences

Empedocles
Stick
Cards
Wizened throngs
Thrown prospective
Strewn
Tantamount
Straddling
Times gone
Potential by
Route resurface
Indistinguishabilities
Ground spectacles
Synonymously
At mount Etna
What
There

- Paul Shapshak, PhD -

Epigramme 600

Shadow Shade

Folded fells hills downs
Farhilted field self
Timed manifested
Stead self-resemblances
Separable separabilities
Semblances
Goneby time
Separate anxiety
Postured
Unheld set
Shade walks
Sevenfold bade moving
Submerged dark works
Shade rank hindered
Shaded shadows

Epigramme 613

Swift Sort

Smilefox
Reign sail hoist
Salve
Salutations
Sated salute
Skyskill
Sardonic saturate
Shadow

- Paul Shapshak, PhD -

Epigramme 307

Fly By

Adamantamine
Colds flu SARS
Panoplies
Pan pipes
Pippin
Stoppin' in
Stalled
Stalted slates
Slater posed
Later

Epigramme 601

Antecedent

Troll vex'd trinket
Strut trolled accomplishment
Accompaniment
Stumbled stubbled
Triumph trifled trimmed
Trammeled travail
Travesty charade
Characterized
Cherry-piqued
Charicatured
Trail tract travelled
Intact
Acreage tract totaled

- Paul Shapshak, PhD -

Epigramme 614

Evanescence

Augur mortgag'd
Lidless sear'd overlooked
Affront'd trod
Antecedent sierra
Mont Blanc
Etna non est

Canzone 603

Worth

Trophies villas arbitrage
Topless towers showered Augur
Icummin in April May June
Ilium sardonic estuary
Tidal illustriousness
Promontory promotion
Sales salubrious inviolabilities
Products distributions
Idyllic bonds hedges
Grown fenced falcons
Eagles condors
Just vultures circling
Mount Kilimanjaro
Swahili Bantu bundu bound
Eastwards quaked visualized
Happenstanced days nights evening tides
Untired by daily push pulls
Capital investitures
Investments hasty
History trash bins clearly
Violet trolling raising capitals
Troll vexed currencies commodious
Triumphant vex'd investing
Vex trinkets surplus yields
Trim vex'd markets
Trifle vest'd futures
Trifl'd vesting excess production
Tried tessellates assets valuations
Blanket derivatives

Epigramme 411

Leige

Meadows' office
Office-hence
Outspokenly maladroit
Leige-betold

PART VIII

HEALTH

Epigramme 305

Everywhere Whom

Neutrinos hither neutrinos
Thither ubiquitous
Neutrinos universal
Globally more summers'
Herein dreamt
In cuminn fraught
Than courteous tolerance
Intradural conscript thought allied
Allayed handles
Tunes fragments conglomeratory
Tuned overtoned consecutively
Diametric synonyms defined
Pronounced consumptions
Parade day
Dissonances befitted harmony
Glass tumbril
Set aright wright corrected sight
Framed dreams hidden dens dispossession

Epigramme 615

Refrain

Six hundred
Thirteen
Refrains reframes each
Dor vador
Tohu vavohu
Circumscribed
Confetti westerns
Convolutions
Voluntaries
Cenotaphs

Canzone 430

Hurricanes Earthquakes N' Things

Wane viral wisp
Wane wither
Walls windy
Wake window
Vail winding
Votary wind
Vocabularies wilt
Tornado trophies violet
Troll vexed
Troll villa
Triumphant vex'd
Vex trinket vex
Trim trophies violet
Trifle vest'd
Trail trifl'd
Vestal tried veneer-shined

Canzone 420

Gird

Gestalt-memory forth
Gestalt relics
Fiber-bundle gentle
Fiber gentle relinquish
Fortune fellow
Fell forlorn
Weltanschauung
Forlorn fells
Isles bright sunny
Retrospectives
Regardless
Innovates innovatives
Surplus worthing
Uncultivated
Kultur zuider zees
Zazen inextential
Non-Jungian
Existentialism
Bu Freudian

- Paul Shapshak, PhD -

Canzone 500

Invisibilities

Impetuoso

Cosecant crisscrossed
Cesuras cardinal points
Encompassed gyres
Gyres tangled threads
Eagle threads wrens visitations
Silken chains threadbare
Warps woofs spun yarns metals
Clotho Lachesis Atropos
Eumenides' paths space time
Alternatives superpositions
Copper bronze iron
Gold silver amethyst
Pearl ruby emerald
Lake-side cheer country balm
County isles
Cluny Petrarca
Billfolds twenties away
Florins guineas
Earthy mounds bounded
Shapely nectar goblets plates
Down set paths trod by day

Epigramme 304

Entangled Photons

Impetuoso

Aversed ardor cavalcade
Awhile dust thoroughfare
Unpaved overturned
Oaks acorns adorned
Falls chasms showering
Hail maelstrom manifested
Shadowed watched firmament
Vocalization irrigation channeled
Stilled waters reflections
Quantum entangled
Photons neutrinos
Still watch towers

Canzone 498

Farm Field

Folk upon glade
Valley meadows
Swept embankments
Mused incandescents
Befell murmurings
Rodinesque quietitudes
Iridescent ornaments
Pallets bedizened ersatz
Counterfeit ethics conscience
Integrity swelled up to banks
Heartfelt loiter utteranced
Lurk falter past vistas panoramas
Outviews censorious
Sanctimonies expansed remote
Idylls scullions tallied tapestries

Canzone 423

Predecessor

Concordian vantage
Conceit vanquish'd
Hillside vanity hid
Vanquish bartered braid
Unblockading vain disputed
Worth token honored upbraided
Winters' toils upgraded
Anodyne perplexity upstaged undined
Undefined distempered dynastic temperance

Canzone 431

Woken

Wall winding

Walls' lair

Kindle contrived

Winter-freeze ebb

Whither viral

Unwarp'd virtue

Wonder warrantise

Upstanding habitat

Catapulted inveigled

Awaken window

Windy wane

Challenge unspontaneous

Wardrobe

Diminish wisp

Warrant'd vista

Warranties contemptuous

Unwaste'd worth scorn

Pleotropic outcomes

Epigramme 303

Imperious

Harrowing bent
Portcullis promulgated
Pomegranates hard fast land
Officiousness meadows brook
Changed agendas reversed reveries
Oft on mind merchandize redeem
Molded primed prosaic bent emancipated

PART IX

CYBERNETIC ALLEGORIES

Epigramme 601

Autonomous Steps

Levels sovereignty
Coordinated coordinates
Miscellaneous variables
Detached selected
Culled arrangement
Color charm differential
Field jacobian
Pale settlement
Buxtehude steps
Hausman allegories
Jung fabled mysteries

Canzone 301

Elocution

Merchandized olden-das
Ornament arrival merit
Opened inception ornament
Opened out-of-time pocket oppression
Oppression fodder out-of-it pluck out-grown
Repressed driven garnish out-of-pocket
Salads excitations word
Innervation ulterior alternative
Imitations excitations

Epigramme 713.5

Comic Travesty In Five And A Half Lines

Worth wasteth not
iWish iDeliver iTruth iTrust
Evinced advantaged improved
Vassaled been there seen that over
Waxeth not error miscalculate
Droll examination star-lighted
Cosmic error fly byes
But not now nowhere never
Nor provoked providence

Canzone 427

Sain Moirai

Deep Domesday morning
Alacrity day
Awoke folk upon dreamscape
Garlanded Rhodes
Skyros protected
Protracted
Thetis foreboding
Islands Donne's
Peeled refrains
Homilies Pelean
Myrmidons
Nereids havens oft seared
Ivied walls
Tenth year
Chryseis supplication
Supplant
Denied Nereids denied
Clotho Lachesis Atropos
A propos last word
Out-of-pocket explanatory calm

Epigrammaton 722

Method

Overall routed   Wending wended
Where-through   Crease west-gated

Epigramme 727

Brusque

Praise-sport posterity outstripped
Parcel predesign panic preposition
Past particle partial prepar'd
Preposterous prepositioned
Penury presume patent perfection
Presume perforce
Daily creditable credible
Terrible perfect drills
Presumptive perish'd
Perjur'd pejorative

- Paul Shapshak, PhD -

Epigramme 302

Hive

Humming threw
Amass argue
Dream argumentation
Late learner steps
Keep kept kempt
By light by day
Night iris bloom field
Betides blunt rheum
Let stand cedar poplar
Live sauropod

Paradox Epigramme 705

Indistinct

Poplar wreath
Breathe cypress
Nighttime chaplet
Clandestine
Garlanded wreath
Forgotten wrath
Unspontaneously articulate

Canzone 600

Tatters

Tattered swell'd
Swerved rested
Tattered syzygy
Swollen taunt
Steel'd dome
Taunt-tainted
Steep taunt-tainted
Termed latitude
Sympathy night
Teacher taught
Sharper sheaves
Tomorrow steeped-up
Showered shed
Shun night beknighted
Beckoned lassitude
Side-bent strained
Sink silent stilled
Wrested

Epigramme 301

Time's Unthrift

Spell'd dazed
Vacancy tiresome
Interest tired
Toiled reputed
Token vain tabled
Bane conceit
Vanquish'd total
Tract vanquish
Tract vantage
Trail vantage unlikeliness
Travail dissimilarity

- Paul Shapshak, PhD -

Epigramme 707

Veneer

Vassalage traveled
Tread vassal
Treasure managed
Treat façade
Trelice veneer-glow
Tried veneer-shine
Trifl'd vest
Trim vexated
Trinket vex'd semblance
Vermeer
Vest'd trifle
Vested forestalled

CANZONE 48

Ledgers

Ledges leaves moderns
Leeses monumentally
Legacies clauses mortal
Leisures tenants
Mortalities lenients

CANZONE 611

Lyre

Lustrous lour'st
Oblivious lure
Muse-time
Line-bare
Nature's lour
O'rexpress
Live assent
Loan needful
Shown tables altars
Feeble locks
Unneglectful

PART X

THE ARTS

Canzone 700

Eine Kleine Chorale

Hillside pastures
Rested relaxed
Reposed
Rien d'antans
Hugen Munen crisscrossed
Ginungagap
And back
Elevated wayed founded

Canzone 711

Rhine Songs

Brook brambles deer
Resonate tuneful overtone
Note air snowy walls perimetric
Law destinations tracks
Decree slowed momentum
Neutrino waterway fields
Overtone tributary
Directive shadows evanescent windows
Tune strings strung
Initial melody harbingers
Condition state fenced
Crowded states affirmed
Strained stated avowed

Canzone 720

Vantage Travail Worth

Trelice cantilever veneer
Veneer-glow
Treat vassalage
Treasure tread
Fell travail forewarn
Feeble featureless f
Foreswear feathers four
Tract foreswear
Frolic fountain glade fauna
Cantileveled force forbid
Forbidden fault
Vantage fault
Fool fatuous
Fate's wrackful fond fair paths
Worthy wax
Wrack laudable
Cantilevered waters well-intentioned
Variations waterfall
Worthier

Canzone 650

Insensate Ineffable Intuition

Entity invoked
Reduction unanticipated unkind
Insensate insinuate
Censorial chactid
Inculcated entranced
Beguiled belabored unafraid
Need outcome curtailed
Inimitable initial inchoated
Insinceriousnessed inferenced intuitive
Redwood circled timed
Goneby by time immemorialed
Timed ghosted paraded partook
Inestimable insinuate

- Paul Shapshak, PhD -

Canzone 655

Stern Magister

Sins stent across vents
Skill sketch stentorian
Stole-dispair storm
Storm-beaten strained
Strange stratified strain
Sturdy style
None subjunctive
Nor suborn'd
Nor svelted
Strewn stronger strings
Strung-sympathy

Epigramme 700

Theatrical

Thrice
Thriftless twinned
Twisted trundly

Canzone 690

Poesie

Outspoken outcast
Outbrave
Portions outfling
Poesy
Possessed
Outthink persimmons out-coat
Pluck roses from garnered fields
Refrains morning glories
Daffodils speaking snapdragons
Refrains air-borne
Dandelion's advices realized

Epigramme 740

Agreement

Arrange file
Promise profile
Bargain vault
Special express
Prosper profound
Weight reflection
Arranged

Epigramme 742

After

Mammoth garden
Deer porpoise
Tortoise Bernie
Bison crocodile
Turtle elephant
Yard buffalo
Alligator stag
Dolphin elk

Canzone 722

Persistence

Perish prevail presumptious presuppose
Persist perjure
Persist prevaricate
Prevail
Pride prize persist'd pride
Pictures perspective
Pious profound print
Production profitless prognosticate pity
Prognosticate pith pit pitch

- Paul Shapshak, PhD -

Canzone 421

Ode

Watersheds epoch salutatory
Hitherto lugubrious days gone
Date twilight prior
Quelled aphorisms afore
Now stands opportune
Saunters timely sway
Comeliness elevate
Abridge abbreviate
Aster binary shallow fields betide
Beattie betake between
Traced trance troubled psychologies
Jungian nightmares transcendent parallaxes
Preterit preamble conscript dual

Canzone 734

Satyre

Derived creations
Convoluted assignations
Conscripted associations
Blindfolded bands
Destiny
Providence

Canzone 742

Raga Tabled

Tabla sitar raga
Sumer est Ur
Banter twixt multifated band
Chat combine
Wheat rye oats barley
Barely

Epigramme 750

Convergence Quality

Quintessential quora serene qualities
Concatenates concentrate convive
Tranquil quiet composed quietly
Qualms alms almagest quandary quick qualities
Zero zone zoom
Calm

- Paul Shapshak, PhD -

Canzone 733

Convisage

Play intervista inferred votive
Quiet grassland aconvivint
Accord con dates
Datum est revisaged
Constant gerontary
Presences shadows suspended
Whereabouts place
Embankments enveloped locate
Placid lagoon strewn shadily
Envisage anticipated

Epigramme 739

Steps

Stepp'n reside
Froze drams punctuated
When Rommel left Egypt reknown
When curtains unfurl
Sails astronomically founded
Beknownst

Canzone 723

Relativistic Hyperspace Canzone

Imperturbable islands collected
Fibers groups sheaving
Density space concrete compacted
Tensor product plowing
Sublime output seried
Congruence neomorphism hyperspacing
Invariant interval construed
Gap constructing
Non-classical quanta juxtaposed
Hyperplanes Medusa particle meeting

Summed foundation ground base
Punted points heaved too
reveries Peripheral
adorations location
Addresses dreamy drolls darn drummed
Reflections baggages reflectors
Tested tests recuperated reviews
Contrite contraries
Reveries peripherals
Holding water brim
Brimming repudiatedly
Replied g'dday
Leibnitz Newton
Jung Freud
Schrodinger Lorentz
Bohm Fitzgerald
Bohr Einstein
Bose Gandhi

Printed in the United States
by Baker & Taylor Publisher Services